BEHIND THE SCENES

SPORT

Frances Ridley

Editorial Consultant – Cliff Moon

RISING STARS

nasen
NASEN House, 4/5 Amber Business Village, Amber Close, Amington, Tamworth, Staffordshire B77 4RP

Rising Stars UK Ltd.
22 Grafton Street, London W1S 4EX
www.risingstars-uk.com

Every effort has been made to trace copyright holders and obtain their permission for use of copyright material. The publisher will gladly receive information enabling them to rectify any error or omission in subsequent editions.
All facts are correct at time of going to press.

First published 2006

Cover design: Button plc
Cover image: Empics
Illustrator: Bill Greenhead
Text design and typesetting: Marmalade Book Design
(www.marmaladebookdesign.com)
Educational consultants: Cliff Moon, Lorraine Petersen and Paul Blum
Technical consultant: Alida Biagi and Fil Antomiazzi
Pictures: Alamy: pages 6, 7, 8, 10, 11, 13, 16, 20, 28, 30, 37
Empics: pages 4-5, 12, 17, 18, 19, 21, 25, 26, 27, 29, 36, 38, 39, 41, 42, 43, 46

British Library Cataloguing in Publication Data.
A CIP record for this book is available from the British Library.

ISBN: 978-1-84680-050-4

Printed by Craft Print International Ltd, Singapore

Contents

The sports industry

Many people dream of playing sport as a professional, but only a few make it.

It takes a lot of hard work and talent.

Being a pro is not the only job in sport!

The sports industry is a big employer so many people have sports jobs.

4

Many people work
as volunteers.

They train as coaches
or referees.

They help out at
sports clubs.

Other people get paid
for working in sport.

They work at leisure
centres and health clubs.

They work in sports medicine
or sports media.

Amateur sport

Keeping fit

Many people do sport to keep fit and have fun.

Leisure centres are good places to go.

Leisure centres often have:

- a swimming pool

- a gym

- squash courts

- fitness studios

- outdoor pitches

- a café.

Leisure centre staff

Job title	Job description
Leisure centre manager	Runs the leisure centre
Swimming instructor	Teaches swimming lessons
Lifeguard	Makes sure swimmers are safe
Fitness instructor	Teaches exercise classes Teaches people how to use the gym
Gym supervisor	Makes sure people use the gym safely
Sports development officers (e.g. tennis development officer)	**Promote** different sports in the local area

Sports clubs

Most sports have clubs at local, regional and national level.

The clubs run league competitions.

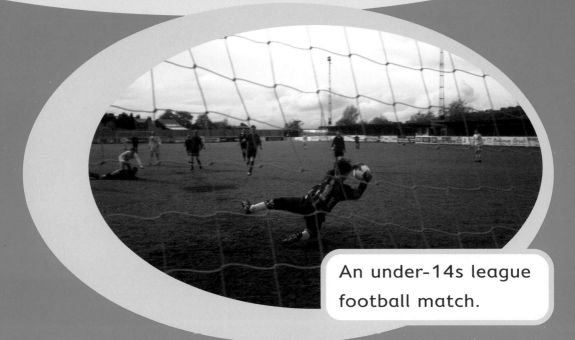

An under-14s league football match.

Volunteer	Job description
Club secretary	Looks after membership Organises events
Coach	Trains club members
Referee	Makes sure sport is played by the rules
Marshall	Helps out at events

Most sports are amateur.

The competitors are not paid.

The staff at sports clubs are **volunteers**.

Learn new skills

Make useful **contacts**

Why volunteer?

Get work experience

Do something you love!

Qualification needed?
No – but you can get one if you want to
Yes – from the sport's **governing body**
Yes – from the sport's **governing body**
No – but you can get one if you want to

Professional sport

Sports professionals are paid to play sport.

Some professionals play team sports — like football or rugby.

Some professionals do **individual sports** — like boxing or athletics.

Being a sports professional is tough.

You have to be:

- **physically** fit — to train or compete every day.

- **mentally** fit — to perform well under pressure.

Most sports professionals have short careers.

It's important to:

- get noticed when you are young

Young boxers from a Boxing Academy.

- train for a second career — just in case!

You can train to be a bricklayer.

Amir Khan

Amir Khan is a professional boxer.

Amir started at the boxing gym when he was 8.

He started boxing in competitions when he was 11.

Did you know?

Amir's cousin is England cricketer Sajid Mahmoud.

In 2004, he won a silver medal at the Olympics.

He was only 17!

Amir turned professional in 2005.

He won his first seven fights.

After his seventh fight, he said he had a lot to learn. But he added:

"I'm getting the hang of being a pro."

Dream Team (Part one)

"Look at this!" said Robert. "How about getting a team together?"

Fareed reached out for the ad. But Jack grabbed it first.

"Great!" said Jack. "I can be the team manager – I'll lead this footie team to victory!"

"Er, hang on," said Robert. "Perhaps the others want to … "

But Jack was already heading for the computer room.

He looked up loads of stuff on the Internet.

Then he went to the kitchen.

"Diet's really important for athletes," Jack told Andy, the cook. "They need carbohydrates, protein and vitamins!"

"I see," said Andy. "But … "

Jack shoved a recipe into his hand. "Cook this for tea!" he yelled as he ran off.

Continued on page 22

Training and team management

Sports coaches

Sports coaches help sports people to reach their **potential**.

A sports coach:

- helps you to keep fit

- teaches you skills and tactics

- **motivates** you to do your best

- gives **feedback** on what you do.

Sometimes coaches have to be tough.

This isn't always easy.

Bill Sweetenham is a top UK swimming coach.

He has a very tough style.

He makes his team work hard and it has had great results.

Training hard at the Olympic holding camp, 2004.

Some people think that Sweetenham is a bully.

But Bill Sweetenham says:

'I set high standards ... I've never been a bully.'

Linford Christie

Many sports professionals become coaches.

Linford Christie was a top Olympic athlete.

Now he coaches some of the best UK athletes.

Linford Christie says:

"Nothing can beat doing it yourself, but the next best thing is helping someone else do it. Before I quit I want to coach an Olympic champion."

Linford Christie coaches Tim Abeyie.

Abeyie won the 60m and the 200m races at the 2006 AAA Indoor Championships.

Only two athletes have ever won both races before – one of them was Linford Christie!

Team managers

Many top coaches become team managers.

Managers are the leaders of their teams.

They make important decisions about players, coaches, sponsors and training.

A good team manager can lead a team to victory.

Clive Woodward was the England rugby team manager.

His team won the 2003 Rugby World Cup!

Woodward's dream team

Manager – Clive Woodward

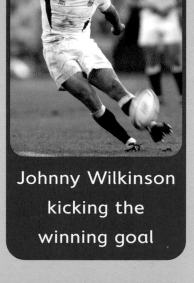

Johnny Wilkinson kicking the winning goal

Team captain – Martin Johnson

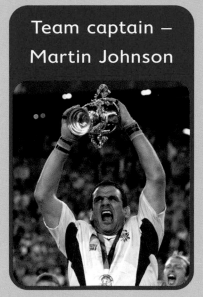

Coach – Andy Robinson

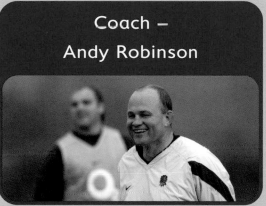

Woodward's secrets for success:

✔ Close teamwork.

✔ Strict diet plan.

✔ Changing into clean shirts at half-time.

✔ Ice baths and eye workouts!

Dream Team (Part two)

Jack got everyone out on the grass.
Only Fareed stayed indoors.

"We need to do some exercises!" said Jack.

He started bending and stretching like
a jack-in-the-box.

"Isn't that a bit fast?" asked Gemma.

"It has to be," said Jack. "We've got loads
to do!"

Fareed watched from a window. He was fed up.

Carol saw him. "What's up?" she asked.

"I don't like Jack bossing me around," he said.

When everyone sat down for tea they were starving.

"It's Saturday!" said Matt. "That means a fry-up!"

Andy came in. He didn't look happy.

He plonked a big dish of bean stew in the middle of the table.

"What's *that*?" asked Gemma.

"It stinks!" said Fareed.

"It's good for you!" said Jack.

He put a big forkful in his mouth. Everyone stared.

"Hmm," said Jack. "It needs some ketchup."

Continued on page 32

Sports medicine

There are many different jobs in sports medicine.

Sports nutritionists

Sports nutritionists advise sports people on diet.

A good diet helps sports people to train and perform well.

Different sports people need different diets.

5% vitamins and minerals – green veg, fruit, milk, nuts

15% protein – red meat, chicken, eggs, cheese

A typical athlete's diet – athletes need to eat a lot of energy foods.

55% carbohydrate foods – pasta, rice, bread, cake

25% fats – cheese, milk, crisps

Sports psychologists

Sports psychologists help sports people to keep **mentally** fit.

Mentally fit athletes:

train and compete at their best

work well as a team

cope well with stress

relax more easily

recover from injury faster

Sports doctors

Sports doctors help sports people to keep healthy.

They help with diet, injury and lifestyle.

They say which medicines
athletes can take before
a competition. Some medicines
show up on drugs tests.

Drugs tests

Sports people are tested for drugs before a competition. This makes the competition fair and stops athletes putting their health at risk.

Dwain Chambers tested positive for drugs in 2003. The UK relay team lost a silver medal and Chambers lost a gold medal. He was banned for two years, from 2004 to 2006.

Sports physiotherapists

Sports physiotherapists are experts in sports injuries.

They help athletes:

- to **prevent** injury.

- to perform at their best – by using their bodies in the right way!

- to recover from injury.

First aid on the pitch for Michael Owen in the 2006 Football World Cup.

Sports physiotherapists use lots of different treatments:

taping

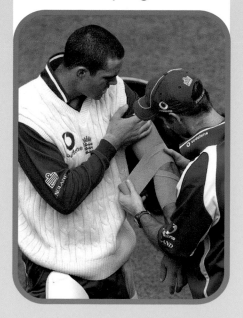

stretching

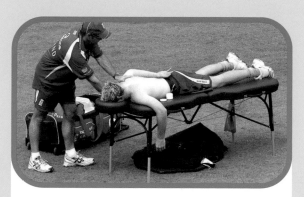

massaging

Metatarsal madness!

Metatarsal bones are long, thin bones in your feet.

Footballers often break them.

Michael Owen, David Beckham and Wayne Rooney have all broken metatarsal bones.

Metatarsal tips!

- Get lots of rest between games.
- Always wear proper sports shoes!

DIY physio!

Unfit fans can injure themselves in a kick around!

The Chartered Society of Physiotherapists has a few tips!

Top five footballing injuries	How it happens	How to **prevent** it
Dislocated shoulder	Saving goals	Don't reach out too fast or too far
Hamstring problems	Sprinting and kicking	Warm up and stretch before you play
Ankle sprain	Falling over	Play on a level pitch
Groin sprain	Kicking, sliding and twisting	Warm up Play on a dry pitch
Dead leg	A heavy blow on the top of the leg	Don't get into heavy tackles!

Dream Team (Part three)

The next morning the nurse went to see Robert.

"It's about Jack," she said. "These exercises have to stop! Gemma has pulled a **hamstring**."

"OK," said Robert.

Ten minutes later, Andy came in.

"It's about Jack," he said. "I am *not* doing any more of his recipes."

"OK," said Robert.

Ten minutes later, Carol came in.

"Don't tell me," said Robert. "It's about Jack. I have to talk to him!"

Jack was fed up.

"What's up?" asked Fareed.

"Nobody does what I say any more," said Jack.

"Look, mate," said Fareed. "You've got some good ideas. But Matt threw up his tea, Gemma pulled her **hamstring** and Kirsty cried when you said her passing was bad."

"I'm a rubbish manager," said Jack.

"No, you're not," said Fareed. "But you have to listen to your team!"

Continued on the next page

Robert went up to Jack's room. He had to say something – but what?

Just outside the door he stopped. Who was that talking and laughing? He put his head round the door.

The football team were in there – and so was Fareed!

Kirsty was doing a warm-up exercise.

"You have to do it *slowly*," she said.

Robert waited for Jack to butt in – but he didn't!

"Everything OK?" asked Robert.

"Fine!" said Gemma. "We're having a team meeting!"

"Great idea!" said Robert. "Did Jack organise it?"

"Yes," said Jack. Then he went red. "But it was Fareed's idea – he's the coach, I'm the manager and Kirsty's the captain."

"Yeah," said Kirsty, "and together we'll lead this team to victory!"

Three weeks later … Jack's team got to the Fairing Fields final – and won!

Referees and umpires

Referees and umpires make sure that sport is played fairly.

They make sure that the players follow the rules.

The rules are set by the sport's **governing body**.

The **governing body** trains the referees and umpires.

Being a referee or umpire is not easy.

Players get angry if they don't agree with a decision.

Referees and umpires have to be firm, calm and fair.

Referees and umpires in professional sport are paid.

Most referees and umpires are volunteers – they do it because they love sport!

Job profiles

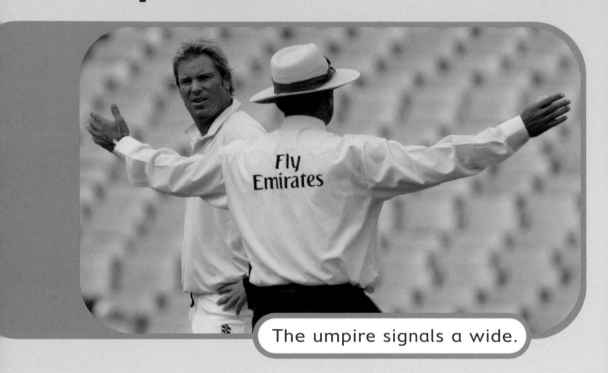

The umpire signals a wide.

Job	Cricket umpires
Rules of game	Laws of Cricket
Position	One near batsman One near bowler
Signals	Hand and arm signals
Duties	Signal **illegal deliveries** Signal when batsman is out Signal when **over** is completed Keep record of deliveries
Dress	Hat, umpire's jacket, trousers, tie

Job	Boxing referee
Rules of game	Rules of the Ring
Position	Inside ring
Signals	Short commands Hand signals
Duties	Stops and starts a **count** Takes points away for fouls Stops fight if boxer is at risk Signals when round is over
Dress	Shirt, bow tie, trousers

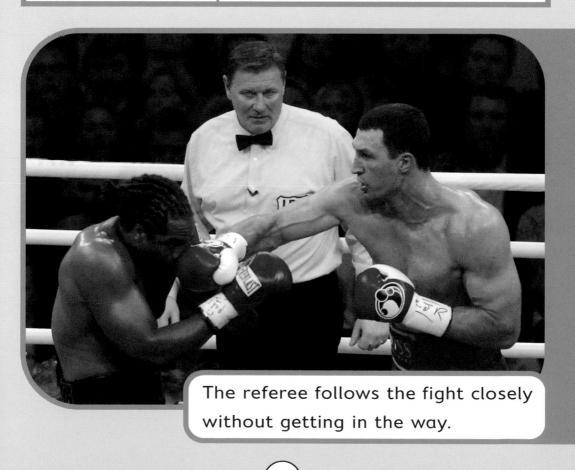

The referee follows the fight closely without getting in the way.

Sports media

The sports media report and comment on sport.

Sports media includes:

- television

- radio

- newspapers and magazines

- the Internet.

Photographers take pictures.

Journalists write **copy**.

What do they do?

Camera crew film sports events.

Sports correspondents present sports reports.

Presenters present sports programmes.

Commentators describe and comment on sports events.

Media fact!

Most commentators and presenters used to be players or managers.

Television companies pay for the right to cover some sports, such as football.

Other sports don't get much **coverage** on television.

As a result, these sports are not as rich as football.

They can't afford huge wages for their players.

Small clubs rely on their fans.

Big football clubs make the most money out of television deals.

They can buy the best players.

As a result, small clubs find it harder to win games.

So it's really important for fans to support their local teams!

Quiz

1   Name five jobs that you can do at a leisure centre.

2   Do you need a qualification to be a coach?

3   In which year did Amir Khan win his silver medal at the Olympics?

4   What is the name of Tim Abeyie's coach?

5   In which year did England win the Rugby World Cup?

6   What are physiotherapists?

7   What are metatarsal bones?

8   Which footballers have broken their metatarsal bones?

9   What injury can you get from saving goals?

10 Where do cricket umpires stand?

Glossary of terms

contacts   Useful people.

copy   The words a journalist writes.

count   The referee counts ten seconds over a fallen boxer – if the boxer doesn't get up, he has lost the fight.

coverage   The amount of time or space given to something in the media.

feedback   Information about your performance – what went wrong, what went right and how to improve.

governing body   Responsible for setting rules, organising events and promoting their sport.

groin   The front of your body at the very tops of your legs.

hamstring   The back of your legs just above your knees.

illegal deliveries   A ball thrown in a way that is against the rules.

individual sports   Sports you compete in on your own.

mentally   To do with the mind.

motivates   Makes you want to do something.

over   Six balls bowled in a row from one end of the cricket pitch.

physically   To do with the body.

potential   The capacity to become really good.

prevent   To stop something from happening.

promote   To bring something to people's notice.

More resources

Books

Olympics (DK Eyewitness)
Chris Oxlade
Published by Dorling Kindersley (ISBN: 0756610834)

Football (DK Eyewitness)
Hugh Hornby
Published by Dorling Kindersley (ISBN: 1405302992)

DVDs

Athens Olympic Review (2004)
All the best bits from the 2004 Athens Olympic Games – plus a
special section on British medal winners!

Really Bend It Like Beckham (2004)
Fremantle Home Entertainment (Cat. No. B00002WYPBY)
David Beckham explains how to recreate his winning skills as he
trains in Madrid.

Magazines

Every local and national newspaper covers sport – and there are
lots of magazines that cover different sports, too. Both these
magazines cover socccr.

World Soccer Magazine and FourFourTwo Magazine

Rugby World
This magazine covers rugby football.

Websites

The BBC Sport website is full of information.
http://news.bbc.co.uk/sportacademy

All the latest results and special pages dedicated to football,
rugby, cricket, golf and Formula One racing, plus news on US
and Irish sports.
http://www.skysports.com

Answers

1 Leisure centre manager, swimming instructor, lifeguard, fitness instructor, gym supervisor

2 Yes – from the sport's governing body

3 2004

4 Linford Christie

5 2003

6 Experts in sports injuries

7 Long, thin bones in the foot

8 Michael Owen, David Beckham, Wayne Rooney

9 Dislocated shoulder

10 Near the batsman and bowler

Index